Ancient Athletes

Haydn Middleton

Game On!

Today, millions of people are so serious about sport, it is like a religion to them. More than 2000 years ago, people were **sport mad** too – and to them it *was* a religion! Sportsmen all over ancient Greece and the Roman Empire pitted their skills against one another as a way of worshipping their gods. Huge crowds gathered to watch the 'Games' and sometimes it was hard to tell just who was being worshipped – the gods or the champion sportsmen!

As you read about some exhausting events, write down and keep your answers to each **QUIZ** question. (Remember, the answers are in the book!) Let the Games begin ...

Sporting champions became dead famous. Their fame was kept alive by statues celebrating their victories.

Programme of Events

Find out who plays, who watches and what rules they have to obey.

PAGES 6 TO 11

Ancient Athlete Do's and Don't's

Find out why this fan risked being executed — just for taking a seat in the stadium!

PAGES 12 TO 13

Toga Trouble

Track and Field Triumphs

Stadium sports that got the fans up on their feet

PAGES 14 TO 17

Fighting for Fun

Hugely-popular one-on-one tests of strength

PAGES 18 TO 23

Wheel Appeal

Hold on to your hats as the horse-drawn chariots hit the track.

PAGES 24 TO 27

Mortal Combat

Into the arena with the gob-smacking gladiators!

PAGES 28 TO 31

Ancient Athlete Do's and Don't's

In ancient Greece and the Roman Empire, there was more to being a top athlete than just being good at sport. You had to stay good through training hard and it was also pretty important to *look* good. Why?

Well, expert sport-watchers liked to group athletes together according to their body types. They believed that an athlete's appearance could hint at the way he would compete. The 'Eagle', for example, could be fierce and strong – but tended to fly away when the going got tough!

The Eagle

Are you a lion or a bear when it comes to sport? If you are a bear, you're slow, but difficult to budge!

The Lion

The Bear

Once the ancient athletes had sorted out 'looking good', they needed to start collecting fans. Ancient sport-lovers were fiercely proud of their local heroes and wealthy citizens would lavish food, gifts and parties on them.

So, the ancient athlete may have had the look and the fans, but there were still more **Do's** and **Don't's** to learn ...

✗ DON'T Cheat

Cheats made the gods seriously unhappy. So, Greek athletes swore an oath to stick to the rules before competing in any Games. If they still fouled, they were punished by whipping-men, or had to pay a big fine.

✗ DON'T Be Female

Sorry girls! There was a strict 'Males Only' rule for competing in ancient Games. Men and boys entered separate competitions, but there were no birth certificates then, so some small men would try to cheat by passing themselves off as boys!

✗ DON'T Worry About The War

Sport was far more important than war! During important Games, the armies would call a truce so athletes could travel and compete in safety. But when the sport was over, the fighting began again!

✓ DO Train Hard

In many ancient towns and cities, there was a big sports complex called a gymnasium for athletes to train in. Sport fans could exercise there too – right alongside their all-time heroes!

✓ DO Eat Right

Trainers and coaches watched their athlete's diet very carefully. Although most ordinary folk could not afford to eat meat regularly, combat athletes needed to gorge on beef, mutton and lamb to put on weight and muscle!

FLESH FACT

Ancient Greek athletes would compete stark naked! And Roman athletes only wore little 'loincloths' to cover themselves. Nude or semi-nude sport would never have caught on in countries with colder climates – like B-tain!

If All That Seems Too Energetic DO Just Watch

An awful lot of people did this! Fifty thousand fans could squeeze into the athletics stadium in Athens, Greece. And at the Circus Maximus in Rome there was room for three times that number! Sport-mad women got a raw deal, though. The only female spectators allowed at the Olympics were priestesses.

★★★★★ when important Games were on.

Toga Trouble

1

Kallipatira was mightily proud of her athletic family. Her father, brothers and nephew were all Olympic combat champions. Now it was the turn of her son, Eukles, to go for glory.

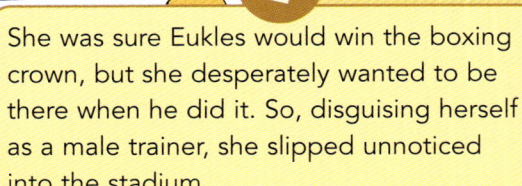

2

She was sure Eukles would win the boxing crown, but she desperately wanted to be there when he did it. So, disguising herself as a male trainer, she slipped unnoticed into the stadium.

3 Eukles did it: he became his family's newest Olympic champion! Going wild with joy, Kallipatira rushed up to her beloved son to hug him – and completely blew her cover.

4 What would the officials do? They had it in their power to have her executed. Instead, out of respect for her famous family, they finally let her off with a warning. But from then on – to keep out any more intruders – Olympic trainers had to be as naked as the athletes!

Track and Field Triumphs

Athletes competed naked in ancient Greek foot races! Twenty or so men would sprint one or two lengths of the stadium, racing only against each other – not against the clock. There was also a long distance race of about four kilometres. This was not nearly as long as our modern marathon of 42 kilometres. Yet the modern marathon *is* named after a famous long run in ancient times …

In 490 BC, a runner was sent to Athens from a place called Marathon, with news that the Greeks had beaten the Persians in battle there. After a run of about 40 kilometres, the runner cried, 'Rejoice. We conquer!' Then he dropped dead of exhaustion. Or so the story goes!

FAST-FORWARD FACT

Long-jumpers carried weights to give them extra forward swing when they took off. Phayllus of Croton once leapt 16.28 metres, sailed over the sandpit and broke his leg on landing!

BOING!

Stadium spectators could also enjoy the thrills and spills of three 'field sports': long-jumping, javelin-throwing and discus-throwing. A champion athlete could not compete at just one of these. He had to beat his rivals in all three, and then win a foot race against them too!

QUIZ When the Greeks beat the ✱✱✱✱✱✱✱✱ in battle,

And still he couldn't claim his winner's crown until he had shown his skills at yet another sport: wrestling. This five-event test of Skill, Speed, Strength and Stamina was called the pentathlon –

Simply Shattering!

Both Greeks and Romans were keen discus-throwers. The discus was first made of stone, then of wood and bronze.

Fighting for Fun

Sportsmen could go to special schools to learn the ancient art of wrestling. Ordinary members of the public, as well as professional athletes, loved to grapple and throw. Wrestling was a skilful sport – yet the rules did allow a wrestler to strangle their opponent until he gave in!

Champion wrestlers became international celebrities. Mighty Milo, from Italy, was famous for tying a string around his forehead, then swelling up the veins in his head to break it! To keep up his strength, Milo kept to an **awesome diet**. He once carried a bull around the Olympic stadium – then chomped his way through the whole beast!

Mighty Milo enjoys the Ultimate Burger Experience!

Have you ever been to a sports event that seemed to go on forever? Ancient boxing matches *could* go on forever! Well, almost. There was no boxing ring, there were no rounds and the contests had no time limit. Ancient boxers had no gloves either! They wrapped their hands in strips of material which left their fingers free. Then they could hold up one finger to show they admitted defeat.

FuNeRaL FaCT

Officials armed with sticks tried to make sure ancient boxers fought fairly. Boxers were supposed only to knock out their opponents, not kill them. But if a boxer did meet his death during a contest, he was immediately declared the winner!

With no time limit, ancient boxers had to be very fit as well as strong. The famous Melankomas of Caria simply used to exhaust his opponent by avoiding either hitting him or being hit. He trained so hard that he was able to hold up his arms, to guard himself from possible attack, for two days!

Ancient crowds flocked to watch boxing and wrestling matches, but 'pankration' was not a combat sport for the sensitive spectator. Pankration fighters could use almost any method to put their opponent down: kicking, breaking fingers, dislocating limbs. In Sparta, there wasn't even a ban on biting or digging out your opponent's eyes! To take part in pankration, sportsmen had to be **super-strong** and **super-fit**, with contests going on until nightfall!

Don't forget, you can bite him!

Pankration means 'complete victory' but, amazingly, the Greeks thought that boxing was the more dangerous sport!

QUIZ Boxers were only meant to ***** out thei

Theogenes of Thasos was an all-time champ at pankration and boxing. In a long and busy career he was victorious at between 1200 and 1400 different sports festivals. No wonder the people of Thasos treated him like a god! After he died, one of his old opponents tried to deface his statue – which toppled over and crushed him!

Wheel Appeal

There was no Greek or Roman Formula One, but ancient sport fans had their own form of high-speed racing: in two-wheeled chariots. Two or four horses drew each chariot lap after lap around a special kind of stadium called a circus.

Greek drivers held the horses' reins, while in Roman racing the reins were tied behind the driver's back. That meant there was no way of controlling the horses' speed, so there were horrific crashes and pile-ups – just like Formula One in fact, only with animals!

Racing chariots were lighter and faster than chariots used on battlefields.

The four-horse chariot race brought great honour to Greek owners, so it is not surprising that champion horses were treated as part of the family.

Fast horses and top-of-the-range chariots were very expensive to look after. Rich Greek owners usually got someone else to do the actual driving – yet after a victory the owner, not the driver, was given the crown!

QUIZ The Romans came from ✶✶✶✶✶. One fiddli

One proud owner, Cimon, won the four-horse race at three different Olympic Games. When his beloved horses died, he had them buried in his own family's grave!

FiDDLeR FaCT

Moody Roman Emperor Nero was said to have played his fiddle while Rome burned. In AD 67 he also fiddled an Olympic crown for himself at chariot racing – despite falling out of his chariot and not finishing the course!

oman Emperor was called ✶✶✶✶.

Mortal Combat

A famous Scottish football manager once joked: 'Football is not a matter of life and death – it's much more important than that!' And for one set of ancient athletes, their sport really was a matter of life and death. By winning their contest, they lived to fight another day. They were, of course, the gladiators of Rome.

> The feverish crowd could sometimes decide if a defeated gladiator should die.

Most gladiators were prisoners of war, slaves or convicted criminals. They trained in special gladiator schools and then had to fight in public two or three times a year. If they survived five years of combat, they could win their freedom.

Gladiators came in many shapes and sizes, and were equipped with a variety of weapons and armour. Fans could easily identify a type known as a 'Samnite' by his large oblong shield, helmet with visor and his short sword. A 'Retarius' only fought with a net and a kind of harpoon for spearing fish! Gladiators did not fight fish, but they did do battle with wild animals. Lions, elephants, bears, deer, goats, dogs and camels were all unleashed into the arena to be 'hunted down' and slaughtered.
Not sport as *we* know it!

Some gladiators became huge heart-throbs. Russell Crowe in the film **Gladiator** became a heart-throb and he didn't do any real fighting!

QUIZ 'Retarius' used a ✶✶✶ to trap his opponent.

FiGHtiNG eMPeRoR FaCT

Some free men loved one-on-one combat so much, they chose to be gladiators. Roman Emperor Commodus trained himself up, fought as a light-armed gladiator – and won hundreds of victories in the arena.

Gladiators would fight their opponents in an ✶✶✶✶✶.